D1253742

STARS OF NASCAR

BY MATT DOEDEN

Reading Consultant:
Barbara J. Fox
Reading Specialist
North Carolina State University

Content Consultant:
Betty L. Carlan
Research Librarian
International Motorsports Hall of Fame
Talladega, Alabama

Capstone
press®

Mankato, Minnesota

Blazers is published by Capstone Press,
151 Good Counsel Drive, P.O. Box 669, Mankato, Minnesota 56002.
www.capstonepress.com

Library of Congress Cataloging-in-Publication Data
Doeden, Matt.
    Kevin Harvick / by Matt Doeden.
    p. cm. — (Blazers. Stars of NASCAR)
    Summary: "Explores the life and racing career of NASCAR Sprint Cup star
Kevin Harvick" — Provided by publisher.
    Includes bibliographical references and index.
    ISBN-13: 978-1-4296-1978-3 (hardcover)
    ISBN-10: 1-4296-1978-3 (hardcover)
    1. Harvick, Kevin — Juvenile literature. 2. Automobile racing drivers — United
States — Biography — Juvenile literature. I. Title.
GV1032.H357D64 2009
796.72092 — dc22
[B]   2007052191

Essential content terms are **bold** and are defined on the spread where they first appear.

Editorial Credits
Abby Czeskleba, editor; Bobbi J. Wyss, designer; Jo Miller, photo researcher

Photo Credits
AP Images/Chris O'Meara, 4–5, 6; Glenn Smith, 7; Mark Humphrey, 14–15
Getty Images for NASCAR/Jamie Squire, 24–25, 26; Jonathan Ferrey, 8–9; Rusty
    Jarrett, cover (car), 22–23, 29
Getty Images Inc./Bill Hall, 27; Chris Graythen, cover (Harvick); Jon Ferrey,
    16–17; RacingOne, 12–13, 18; Rusty Jarrett, 21
Shutterstock/Anastasios Kandris (speed and racing icons, throughout); Bocos Benedict
    (abstract digital background, throughout); Margo Harrison, 10–11; Rzymu (flag
    background, throughout)

1 2 3 4 5 6 13 12 11 10 09 08

TABLE OF CONTENTS

A PHOTO FINISH

Fans at Daytona International Speedway were on their feet. It was the last lap of the 2007 Daytona 500. Kevin Harvick's number 29 car battled for the lead with several other cars.

The leaders roared down the *frontstretch*. Several cars crashed behind them. Smoke and the sound of screeching tires filled the air.

frontstretch — the straight part of the track that includes the finish line

TRACK FACT!

Clint Bowyer's car was in the last-lap crash at the 2007 Daytona 500. His car skidded across the finish line upside down!

Kevin Harvick barely noticed the crash. He was inches behind leader Mark Martin. With a final burst of speed, Kevin crossed the finish line. He won the race by less than 4 feet (1.2 meters)!

Kevin's finish at the 2007 Daytona 500 was the closest finish in Daytona 500 history.

RACING ROOTS

Kevin Harvick was born December 8, 1975, in Bakersfield, California. His parents bought him a *go-kart* when he finished kindergarten. From that day, Kevin wanted to race.

go-kart — a small, lightweight race car

go-kart racing

TRACK FACT!

Kevin raced go-karts for 10 years.
He won nine go-kart championships.

In 1992, Kevin started racing stock cars in NASCAR's *Featherlite* Southwest Series. He spent the next seven years in the lower series of NASCAR. He won the Winston West Series title in 1998.

featherlite — a type of lightweight stock car with a less powerful engine than a regular stock car

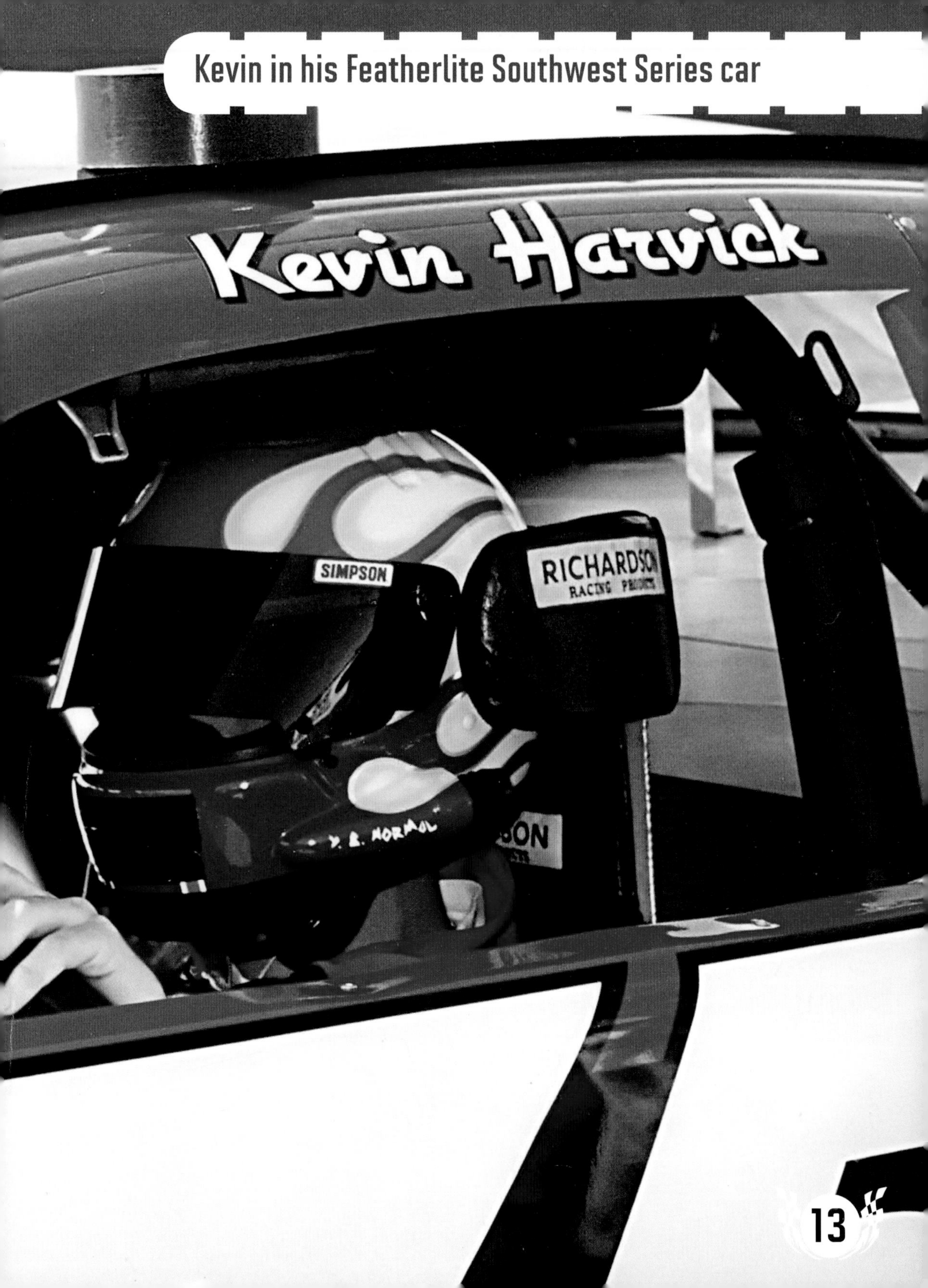

Kevin in his Featherlite Southwest Series car

Car owner Richard Childress saw Kevin race. He offered Kevin a job driving a *Busch Series* car. Kevin impressed him by winning the 2000 Busch Series Rookie of the Year award.

TRACK FACT!

Kevin set two Busch Series Rookie records in 2000: Most Points Overall (4,113) and Most Money Won ($995,274).

Busch Series — NASCAR's second-highest level of competition where drivers gain experience before moving on to the Cup Series

MOVING UP

In 2001, NASCAR legend Dale Earnhardt Sr. died in a crash at the Daytona 500. Childress owned Earnhardt's car. Childress asked Kevin to be his new driver.

Kevin with his 2001 Busch Series championship trophy

The 2001 season was busy for Kevin. He raced full-time in both the Busch and *Cup Series*. He won the Busch Series championship. Kevin also won the Cup Series Rookie of the Year award.

Cup Series — NASCAR's highest level of competition

Winning wasn't always easy for
Kevin. He won just three Cup races
over the next four seasons. He was
frustrated. His temper sometimes
got him in trouble.

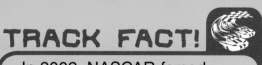

TRACK FACT!

In 2002, NASCAR forced
Kevin to sit out a race
because of rough driving.

But in 2006, Kevin had a great year. He won five Cup races and finished fourth in the **Chase for the Cup**. He also raced full-time in the Busch Series. His nine wins earned him a second Busch Series championship.

Chase for the Cup — the final 10 races of the Cup Series season in which the top 12 drivers battle for the championship

KEVIN TODAY

Kevin's 2007 season started out with a bang at Daytona. First, he won the Busch Series Orbitz 300 race at Daytona. Kevin also won the Daytona 500. But the Daytona 500 was his only Cup win of the season.

Kevin is one of NASCAR's most popular drivers. His fearless style reminds some of the great Dale Earnhardt Sr. Kevin hopes to one day have as much success as Earnhardt.

Kevin Harvick after winning the AMD at The Glen in 2006

Dale Earnhardt and his 1994 Cup championship trophy

Kevin Harvick's Cup Statistics

Year	Races	Wins	Poles	Top-5	Top-10	Winnings
2001	35	2	0	6	16	$3,716,633
2002	35	1	1	5	8	$3,748,105
2003	36	1	1	11	18	$4,994,249
2004	36	0	0	5	14	$4,739,012
2005	36	1	2	3	10	$4,970,049
2006	36	5	1	15	20	$6,201,578
2007	36	1	0	4	15	$7,494,593
Career	**250**	**11**	**5**	**49**	**101**	**$35,864,219**

29

GLOSSARY

Busch Series (BUSH SEER-eez) — NASCAR's second-highest level of competition where drivers gain experience before moving on to the Cup Series; in 2008, the series became the Nationwide Series.

Chase for the Cup — the last 10 races of the Cup season in which the top 12 drivers battle for the championship

Cup Series — NASCAR's highest level of competition; the series has been known as the Winston Cup and the Nextel Cup; it is now called the Sprint Cup.

featherlite (FETH-ur-lite) — a type of lightweight stock car with a less powerful engine than a regular stock car

frontstretch (FRUHNT-strech) — the straight part of the track that includes the finish line

go-kart (GOH-kart) — a small, lightweight race car

impress (im-PRESS) — to make someone think highly of you

rookie (RUK-ee) — a first-year driver

title (TYE-tuhl) — an award given to the champion of a sport

READ MORE

Eagen, Rachel. *NASCAR.* Automania! New York: Crabtree, 2007.

Kelley, K. C. *Racing to the Finish: Teamwork at 200 MPH!* All-Star Readers. Pleasantville, N.Y.: Reader's Digest Children's Books, 2005.

Pristash, Nicole. *Kevin Harvick.* NASCAR Champions. New York: Rosen, 2009.

INTERNET SITES

FactHound offers a safe, fun way to find Internet sites related to this book. All of the sites on FactHound have been researched by our staff.

Here's how:
1. Visit *www.facthound.com*
2. Choose your grade level.
3. Type in this book ID **1429619783** for age-appropriate sites. You may also browse subjects by clicking on letters, or by clicking on pictures and words.
4. Click on the **Fetch It** button.

FactHound will fetch the best sites for you!

INDEX